HOPE
IN THE
VALLEY

PENELOPE BOURDILLON

Illustrated by Marcia Gibson-Watt

Wherever I go I will meet you,
Till you draw your last breath
In this birthplace known as DEATH
Yes, wherever I go I will meet you

Lighting a Candle

When we have gone, it stays alight,
Kindling in the hearts and minds of others
The prayers we have already offered for them,
And for others; for the sad, the sick,
And the suffering—and prayers for
THANKFULNESS too.

HOPE
IN THE
VALLEY

A COMPANION IN TIMES
OF BEREAVEMENT

PENELOPE BOURDILLON

Illustrations by
MARCIA GIBSON-WATT

By the same authors
The Four Graces
A.C.T.S I

Also By Penelope Bourdillon
How God Peel an Onion
God's Abundance

Copyright © 2021 Penelope Bourdillon

Paperback: 978-1-63767-180-1
eBook: 978-1-63767-181-8
Library of Congress Control Number: 2021910535

Research and text © Penelope Bourdillon 2008
Illustrations © Marcia Gibson-Watt 2008

We are indebted to Mr. Len Elliott who so
graciously gave his time and expertise.
Scripture quotations are taken from the Holy
Bible, New International Version.
Copyright © 1973, 1978, 1984 by International Bible Society.

Ordering Information:

BookTrail Agency
8838 Sleepy Hollow Rd.
Kansas City, MO 64114

Printed in the United States of America

I dedicate this book to the future of the Christian Centre for Rural Wales.

Bereavement is a universal and integral part of our experience of love. It follows death as normally as marriage follows courtship or as Autumn follows Summer. It is not a truncation of the process but one of its phases; not the interruption of the dance, but the next figure.

Queen Elizabeth II said after the terrorist attack in New York that

Grief is the price we pay for love.

LLANGASTY CHURCH

PART 1 - THE PARTING

PREFACE

There are many books on bereavement full of cheering verses and charming poems and heart-stopping homilies. There is probably no need for another book on the subject, but I am going to make this into a personal journey which I made after the death of my husband Mervyn, in the hope of reaching someone's broken heart, or at least helping them through what can be a very rough patch.

One thing is certain: until you have trodden the path yourself you have absolutely no idea of what it will be like. I was confident that I would mourn deeply for a given time, then dry my tears, staunch the wound and carry on with a fixed smile on my face. After all I "have God" so, in the words of that glorious song 'I'll never walk alone'. That may be, but I wanted God with a skin on.

Even now after nearly six years I still have pangs of overwhelming grief which flood over me when I least expect it. They have happened in a supermarket when I saw Crunchy Nut Flakes (Mervyn's favourite) or on the Motorway for no apparent reason; even sitting with the family watching Chitty Chitty Bang Bang with silent tears pouring down my face because it was so beautiful and I wanted him to be there to see the grandchildren's shining eyes.

THE JOURNEY

So come with me on the journey, which will not be the same for you, but if it helps any single person with the rocky time ahead of them I shall have fulfilled my purpose. I must warn you that it **is** a stony path, but remember always that God has provided you with tough boots with which to walk it: in other words He will be there with you in the hard times. He **never** gives us more than we can cope with, but we have to learn to trust in Him. He will not take away the pain but He will help you to bear it, and He can even use your suffering for good.

See *Romans 8 :* [38] 'I am convinced that neither death nor life, neither angels nor demons, neither the present nor the future, nor any powers, neither height nor depth, nor anything else in creation, will be able to separate you from the love of God that is in Christ Jesus'.

A friend wrote to me at that time saying: "The storm rages but Jesus is asleep in the bows of the boat. In the storm live in the Psalms. Let the Word of God be your strength and your song. Satan hates Christians who praise God in the fiery furnace. Have no thought for tomorrow. Release everything into God's hands. He is faithful and so merciful. You are such a precious pearl in His sight, and He is so proud of His children who laugh at the waves of affliction which all end up as bubbles on the beach…" Good stuff!

Of course everyone finds their own way along the road, but maybe the best and simplest advice is to put your hand into the hand of God. If you can do this and trust in him, He will guide you and lead you.

The first thing you have to face is the abject misery of the actual parting. I remember describing it to a friend as being torn in two, limb by limb: no neat division with a sharp knife. I also remember feeling physically sick sometimes.

Just as he showed us something about suffering and sickness and dying in his last days alive, in death Pope Paul II showed us something about grieving and taking our leave. The good death, good grief, good funerals come from keeping the vigils, from bearing our burden honourably, from honest witness and remembrance. They come from going the distance with the ones we love.

Thomas Lynch

LETTING GO

This page is to be centred upon death itself and helping your loved one to cross the threshold…

It is useful to remember that hearing is the last sense to go, so it is worth talking even when they are seemingly unconscious. I wish I had taken more note of this at the time.

A good prayer to say for the departed:

.... *(Name)*
Go forth upon the journey from
this world, O Christian soul,
In the name of God the Father who created you. In
the name of Jesus Christ who suffered for you. In the
name of the Holy Spirit who strengthened you.

May the Angels of God support you
on your journey to eternity
May your portion this day be in peace, and
thy dwelling in the heavenly Jerusalem.

May you find eternal rest with ....
(name any loved ones who have already departed)
And the host of loved ones who have gone before you.

Well done thou good and faithful servant,
enter thou into the joy of thy Lord.

DEATH

We seem to give them back to thee, O God who gavest them to us. Yet as thou didst not lose them in giving, so do we not lose them by their return.

Not as the world giveth, givest thou, O lover of souls. What thou givest thou takest not away, for what is thine is ours also if we are thine.

And life is eternal and love is immortal, and death is only an horizon, and an horizon is nothing save the limit of our sight.

Lift us up, strong Son of God that we may see further; cleanse our eyes that we may see more clearly, draw us closer to thyself that we may know ourselves to be nearer to our loved ones who are with thee.

And while thou dost prepare a place for us, prepare us also for that happy place, that where thou art we may be also for evermore.

Bishop Brent

Death is a door that enables our loved ones
to move from a lesser to a greater realm.

FACE IT AND FEEL IT

The first thing to do when confronted by a disaster or loss is to face it and feel the pain caused by it, but remember that you cannot begin to rebuild a crumbling wall unless first you are willing to mourn over it.

O God help me to grieve over the loss in my life, and help me realise that facing and feeling the emotions that arise within me is not a sign of faithlessness.

The sooner one can grasp the reality of your grief, the sooner you can begin the grief journey.

These first three lines of a Gerard Manley Hopkins poem takes us straight to the bottom of the pit, which is the only place to start:

> No worst, there is none.
> Pitched past pitch grief
> More pangs will,
> schooled at forepangs,
> wilder wring.
> Comforter, where,
> where is your comforting?

Emily Dickinson takes us through a harrowing time; the only thing one can do is to face up to the funeral and I am sure that one is given extra help to get through it. I had not prepared myself for the first sight of the coffin, and I remember thinking that my legs were going to buckle under me . . .

> I felt a funeral in my brain
> And mourners to and fro
> Kept treading, treading till it seemed
> That sense was breaking through.
>
> And when they all were seated,
> A service like a drum
> Kept beating, beating till I thought
> My mind was going numb.
>
> And then I heard them lift a box
> And creak across my soul
> With those same boots of lead, again
> Then space began to toll.
>
> As all the heavens were a bell,
> And Being but an ear,
> And I and silence some strange race,
> Wrecked, solitary, here.

Emily Dickinson

I have desired to go
    Where springs not fail,
To fields where no sharp and sided hail
    And a few lilies blow.

And I have asked to be
    Where no storms come,
Where green swell is in the havens dumb,
    And out of the swing of the sea.

Gerard Manley Hopkins

I am sure that many of us have thought how good it would be to run away to a safe place where 'no storms are', but we must be brave and keep on however tough the going is.

We can almost sense the departed speaking to us.

Remember me when no more day by day
You tell me of our future that you planned:
Only remember me, you understand
It will be late to counsel then or pray.
Yet if you should forget me for a while
And afterwards remember, do not grieve:
For if the darkness and corruption leave
A vestige of the thoughts that once I had,
Better by far you should forget and smile
Than that you should remember and be sad.

Christina Rossetti 1830-1894

DEATH BY SUICIDE

What some people have to endure is dreadful and of course everybody deals with grief in their own way. I was very fortunate when Mervyn died that there were no skeletons in the cupboard; also the family were all wonderful and so were my friends. I feel that people who are left by their husband or wife have a dreadful row to hoe; likewise anyone who has lost someone as a result of suicide. The next three pages are on this subject because I think it is horribly necessary in these sad and worrying times.

My heart bleeds for the nearest and dearest who are left behind after someone has taken their own life. I am sure that we can pray for the departed with effect, and that we will meet them in heaven, but inevitably there are so many "If only's." Don't beat yourself up if you are the one left behind. So remember to put your pain to work. If you can see no other purpose, then at least God can cause your experience to comfort others.

This was written by someone who had lost a son who took his own life: . . .

> Only God knows what this
> child of his suffered in the
> silent skirmishes that took
> place in his soul. But our
> consolation is that God does
> know - and understands.

I hope this prayer may give consolation when required:

God of all consolation, grant to
those who grieve,
the spirit of faith and courage,
that they may have
the strength to meet the days to come
with steadfastness and patience,
not grieving without hope,
but trusting in your goodness;
Through him who is the resurrection
and the life, Jesus Christ our Saviour,
Amen.

The Bible is full of people who for different reasons found life too much.

Try reading Job for instance, and of Paul's sufferings in *2 Corinthians; see chapter 1 3 : 6.* Tell God how you feel: He is the Father of compassion and the God of all comfort. He will 'comfort us in all our troubles, so that we can comfort those in any trouble with the comfort we ourselves have received from God . . .'

Only today someone pointed out to me that one cannot live on the mountain tops, and in any case roots only grow in the valleys. So take heart in your suffering if this is for you. Maybe you will help others in time.

Another Prayer that I hope might be useful:

> We pray for release from guilt,
> that our sorrow may be free
> from self-blame and bitter regrets.
>
> Pour out your compassion and
> cleansing love wherever the ripples
> of hurt and guilt have spread.
>
> We commend
> (Name) ………………..………......…..
> into your strong and loving hands.
>
> You are the one who knows him
> through and through.
> We trust in your goodness,
> compassion and infinite love.
>
> Take us all into your loving purposes
> and cleanse us from hopeless grief
> and self-punishing pain.
>
> Help us to mourn in hope of ultimate
> healing and release. Through
> Jesus Christ our Lord.

A word of warning: don't **ever** be tempted to consult a medium . . .

'Let no-one be found among you who is a medium or spiritist or who consults the dead. (It) is detestable to the Lord.'

Deutoronomy 18 : 10-11

HUMOUR

So we have stared death in the face. We have accepted the truth, which is vitally important. Now we must learn how to cope with the next stage, but, before we go into the second section, I want to stress how important it is to mourn. I don't mean to be facetious by including the following poem, but I hope it will bring a smile to your lips, as it does to mine, even when ones heart is breaking.

Stop all the clocks

Stop all the clocks, cut off the telephone,
Prevent the dog from barking with a juicy bone,
Silence the pianos and with muffled drum
Bring out the coffin, let the mourners come.
Let aeroplanes circle moaning overhead
Scribbling on the sky with the message He Is Dead.
Put crepe bows round the white necks of
the public doves,
Let the traffic policemen wear black cotton gloves.
He was my North, my South, my East and West,
My working week and my Sunday rest,
My noon, my midnight, my talk, my song;
I thought that love would last for ever:
Was I wrong?

W. H. Auden

SORROW

Our times of depression may have other causes but we must not feel guilty if we feel low. Soon after Mervyn died, I thought that people must be thinking 'Why is she such a misery because surely if she believes in this God then should He not uphold her?'

It is perfectly in order for Christians to mourn and to feel miserable. They are in no way exempt from the process of grief; there is no superhuman way out of depression. The difference is that they have the tools with which to cope. I suggest that the most important thing you can do is to reach for your Bible and open it: read it daily; study it; read commentaries on it; let God speak to you through it. George Bernard Shaw said that although it was written all those years ago it is still as up to date as the morning's newspaper. The important truth to know is that God's Word gives strength and comfort and hope.

'Garlands instead of ashes;
Gladness instead of mourning;
Praise instead of despair.'

Isaiah 61 : [3]

JOY

...need to feel guilty if you are joyful. ...ced by Christians is not superficial ...t, I remember feeling a deep sense of ...e first dark days of loss. Someone told me ... t my joy would not be taken away. I do not know how I would have kept going without it.

I was perhaps fortunate not to feel any anger, but there were the inevitable feelings of shock, numbness and disbelief. I could scarcely take it in that Mervyn had left me. He always said that we could face anything together, and I remember feeling almost hurt that he could have gone away without me. For over forty years we had done so much together and now I was on my own. It was almost impossible to realise this in its full extent at first. However I had affirmation that he was in the right place, which was the greatest blessing of all.
Praise the Lord!

'You will Grieve, but your Grief will Turn to Joy'

John 16 : 20

CHILDREN

Seamus Heany wrote what I consider an immortal line: *"(children) could stream through the eye of a needle"*. So let us for a short space look at some children's thoughts, remembering Jesus' command *'Let the children come unto me.. for the Kingdom of God belongs to these'. Luke 18 :16* We can learn so much from them even, or perhaps especially, in our hours of darkness, so if you are able to spend time with little people whether they are grandchildren or other people's children, consider yourself very blessed. They do not let you become introspective, so allow yourself to smile and laugh (however much it may hurt at first) and take joy in their funny sayings and doings. For this reason here are two light-hearted little poems, which you may not be in the mood for yet. I hope that in time you will enjoy them. Be aware of how much we can learn from the innocence of children:

Children's song

We live in our own world, a world that is too small For you to stoop and enter even on hands and knees: The Adult Subterfuge.
And though you probe and pry with analytic eye, And eavesdrop all our talk with an amused look, You cannot find the centre where we dance, where we play, Where life is still asleep under the closed flower, Under the smooth shell of eggs in the cupped nest That mock the faced blue of your remoter heaven.

R.S. Thomas

I couldn't resist this when I read it in Ireland and I think it should be entitled ADVICE FROM YOUNG CHILDREN.

Advice to young children

"Children who paddle where the ocean bed shelves steeply Must take great care they do not paddle too deeply."

Thus spake the awful ageing couple Whose hearts the years have turned to rubble.

But the little children, to save any bother, Let it in at one ear and out at the other.

Stevie Smith

PART 2 - THE GRIEVING PROCESS

Lord, take these tears, mortality's relief
And till we share your joys forgive our grief.

Alexander Pope

To mourn too long for those
we love is self-indulgent.
But to honour their memory
with a promise to live a little better
for having known them
gives purpose to their life
and some reason for their death.

This may sound trite but I do feel that we are sometimes over anxious about death. I think we should consider it more as Corrie Ten Boom said, that it is like an old retainer waiting to welcome us in their comfortable arms.

THE FINE VEIL

Titian's sublime picture entitled *Noli me Tangere* shows Mary trying to touch Jesus after the Resurrection: He is gently rejecting her, saying *"Do not touch me."* I stood in front of it with silent tears pouring down my face after Mervyn had died. It may only be a very fine veil that divides us, but as far as I was concerned it might as well have been the Berlin wall.

However I do like the idea of the door being ajar; so near and yet so far:

He is not lost,
Our dearest love,
Nor has he travelled far;
Just stepped inside
Home's loveliest room
And left the door ajar.

Canon Scott Holland

WHERE IS GOD?

The ever present question one hears is 'Where is God?' or 'Why does He allow bad things to happen?' This is a huge subject, but remind yourself that He is there with you in the boat that is being tossed on a stormy sea. It is so often through our suffering that we draw close to Him. He uses bad situations to bring about good. I like the analogy that if we stay in the harbour He cannot help us: it is only when we have the courage to leave the harbour (our comfort zone) that He can steer the boat. So take that first step of faith like Peter getting out of the boat.

> I was falling down into a pit of fear
> and grief and hopelessness. He was not there -
> for I could not sense His presence,
> see His face or feel His loving care.
> I fell deeper still;
> The darkness overwhelmed my soul
> with inexpressible alarms
> but waiting there for me, I found -
> His everlasting Arms!

B. Kaye Jones

'The Lord is close to the broken-hearted and saves those who are crushed in spirit.'

Psalm 34 : 18

GUILT

I have astonished myself recently by rejoicing in the book of Leviticus: guilt is dealt with under the old law when sacrifices were ongoing. However, Old Testament sacrifices are no longer needed. We now have the Cross of Jesus which is a once-for-all Sacrifice: He is the Scapegoat. This throws up big words like Substitution but that needs a whole book of its own. The only answer to guilt is to accept that Jesus died for our sins: yours and mine.

God is the God of salvation, justice and mercy which were all seen at the Cross.

> Let us draw near to God with a sincere heart in full assurance of faith, having our hearts sprinkled to cleanse us from a guilty conscience.

God takes sin seriously. However there is no need to beat yourself up because your loved one has died. This is important. Do not blame yourself - or anyone else - for their death; nothing is more detrimental than blame, which so often turns to bitterness and resentment.

So change your mindset if you are wallowing in self pity and think of the blessings that have been bestowed upon you. Maybe you hadn't even noticed, because you were so wrapped up in self pity. (I know. I've been there. I thought my heart was going to break).

This can be tough, but remember that He has given you the tools. He wants our hearts, not sacrifices. The only sacrifices that we are now required to bring to the Lord are sacrifices of praise and thanksgiving. So what is stopping you?

"Count your many blessings; name them one by one, and it will surprise you what the Lord hath done."

COMFORT

The Epistles are also a great source of comfort: look at Paul's anguish in 2 Corinthians chapter 4:

'We are hard pressed on every side, but not crushed, perplexed, but not in despair; persecuted, but not abandoned; struck down, but not destroyed'.

As we grow older our bodies are gradually dying, but we ourselves are being made stronger each day. These troubles are preparing us for eternal glory when our troubles will seem like nothing. Our bodies are like tents that we live in here on earth. But when these tents are destroyed God will give us homes in heaven that will last for ever. *Read the rest of chapter 4, especially verses 16-18 and chapter 5 : 1*

'Blessed are those who mourn for they will be comforted'

Matthew 5 : 5

FEELINGS

We need feelings in every situation, perhaps even more than usual in times of suffering.

"Don't be afraid of your feelings: feelings are not necessarily the enemy of faith. Handled rightly they are faith's great ally."

Roy Clements

Give sorrow words. The grief that does not speak whispers the o'erfraught heart and bids it break.

Macbeth

Allowing the pain of grief means facing the feelings and the memories both good and bad. It means acknowledging our emotions as real and valid and allowing ourselves to feel out of control. Healing can then begin.

When Christ shall come with shout of acclamation
And take me home, what joy shall fill my heart;
Then shall I bow in humble adoration,
And there proclaim: my God, how great Thou art.

Karl Boherg

GRIEF

Grief is like a long winding valley where any bend may reveal a totally new landscape. Not every bend does. Sometimes the surprise is the opposite one: you are presented with exactly the same sort of country you thought you had left behind miles ago. That is when you wonder whether the valley isn't a circular trench. But it is not. There are partial recurrences, but the sequence doesn't repeat.

> 'Though He brings grief,
> He will show compassion,
> so great is His unfailing love....'

Lamentations 3 : 32

When is mourning over? Have I finished? I realise now, in my sixth year, that mourning is probably never 'finished'. But one gets better at coping with it, and it is not quite so agonisingly painful. It can still strike unexpectedly though.

> Say not in grief that they are no more,
> but in thankfulness that they were.

THE SHIFTING TRIANGLE

I remember being told by an elderly relative when Mervyn and I were engaged that marriage was a triangle: the best marriages are like a triangle with God at the top. When the first of the couple dies, the triangle is still intact. The apex has shifted and there are now two at the top: God and the departed loved one.

Another huge comfort I found was this prayer which was said at our wedding in 1961, and then at the Thanksgiving Service for Mervyn:

The God of Heaven so join you now, that you may be glad of one another all your lives; and when He which hath joined you together shall separate you, may He again stablish you with an assurance that He hath but borrowed one of you for a time to make both more perfect in the Resurrection, through Jesus Christ our Lord.

ADJUSTING

This is perhaps the most difficult thing of all. I had seldom had a meal on my own so I found this a huge stumbling block and for months I would get two plates out of the cupboard when I wasn't thinking. I try to read or write while I am eating otherwise I eat far too fast and get on with the next job. But you get used to anything in time, and one good thing is that you can eat whenever you like. Cold comfort but it is a bonus.

It is good to have interests - and projects too. I have had too much to do, some of my own making. I suppose I quite like a challenge and I have been endlessly involved with builders over these past years. I am still trying to make a garden out of a derelict site which is a prodigious task. But I miss Mervyn coming out to plead with me to stop gardening when it was getting late, and saying there was a glass of wine awaiting me. I did love being cherished - I am sure we all do. I miss doing the cherishing too, but again I say that one must not wallow in self pity, after all there is eternity to look forward to. Alleluya!

Here is a warning against self-pity which is worth learning from the birds:

> I never saw a wild thing sorry for itself.
> A small bird will drop frozen from a bough
> Without ever feeling sorry for itself.

> *D.H.Lawrence*

TIME

The other huge issue is time because I guess that no-one wants too muchtime on their hands to sit and think. It is one of the devil's wiles to make us frenetic, and it is only too easy to become busier than we need to be.

Gone are the days that Granny was looked after and expected to be fairly sedentary; I always smile when I think of Noel Coward's song "What's going to happen to the children when there aren't any more grown ups." Even in my eighties I don't feel very 'grown up'! However I am working towards having more time to read and try to be still.

> May time soften the pain until all that remains
> is the warmth of the memories …
> and the love that you shared.

There is no doubt that time does heal and soften your pain, but no-one can do it for you. People can help of course, both by prayer and practical assistance, but you cannot take any short cuts on the journey marked grief, and you just have to walk it alone - and yet never alone, because God is **always** there to call upon day and night. He never puts on the answerphone and goes away.

A Sundial Motto

Time is

Too slow for those
who Wait
Too swift for those
who Fear
Too long for those
who Grieve
Too short for those
who Rejoice.
But for those who Love

Time is not.

THE VALLEY OF WEEPING

When they walk through the valley weeping they will continue to grow stronger.

(From Psalm 84)

When you lose what you love you go through five main stages:
The first is **denial:**
 'No, it can't be happening to me'.
The second is **anger:**
 'God, why are you allowing this to happen?'
The third is **bargaining:**
 'Please make it go away.'
The fourth is **depression:**
 This leads to silence and withdrawal.
The fifth is **acceptance:**
 'Not my will but Thine be done.'

Whether it's the loss of a child, a marriage, a job, your health etc., when you turn to God He'll give you the grace to embrace it, grieve it, express it, release it, and go on to become stronger.

Sometimes we seek quick relief by releasing it before we've gone through these stages. That is because we fear the process. We have been taught that any show of emotion is a show of weakness, so we hide it. But we only stuff it into our emotional garbage can, then spend all our time and energy sitting on the lid, trying to keep the contents from spilling out.

It is knowing and embracing the truth, including its painful aspects, that sets you free. You must be willing to forgive. But until you come to grips with the enormity of your loss, including any injustice of what was done to you, you are not ready to forgive. When you rush to forgive, you forgive only in part and you are released only in part.

I took the above piece from Word for Today which is an excellent daily devotional produced by United Christian Broadcasters. It often touches the spot, and I recommend it.

Are you running away from pain today? Are you trading it in prematurely for some other feeling? That is not God's way. Jesus said: 'You will weep and mourn.., but your grief will turn to joy... now is your time of grief, but I will see you again and you will rejoice, and no-one will take away your joy.'

John 16 : 20-22

'Then you will know the truth,
and the truth will set you free.'

John 8 : 32

BOUGHROOD CHURCH

PART 3 - TRUST IN GOD

We have been at the bottom of the pit and may be in a state of misery and depression. The Psalms are a perfect place to begin the next stage of the journey. Turn to Psalm 42 and 43 which deal with depression and read them through several times as one piece of writing. Note the desperate pleas, such as:

> 'I say to God my Rock,
> "Why have you forgotten me?
> Why must I go about mourning,
> oppressed by the enemy?"

also the refrain that repeats:

> 'Why are you downcast, O my soul?
> Why are you so disturbed within me?
> Put your hope in God,
> For I will yet praise Him,
> My Saviour and my God'.

The key word is HOPE, but more of that later.

> 'The Lord is close to the broken-hearted and
> saves those who are crushed in spirit'.

Psalm 34 : 18

However unfamiliar you are with the psalms, I am sure that you know God's beautiful promise in number 23: 'Though I walk through the valley of the shadow of death, I will fear no evil, for you are with me; your rod and staff, they comfort me…'

I love David Pawson's suggestion that we should treat Psalms 22, 23 and 24 as a sandwich as they fit together so beautifully. He calls them the cross, the crook and the crown: they present us with a Lord who is first of all a Saviour, then Shepherd, and then Sovereign. And we are allowed to call him our friend. What a friend to have!

'The sacrifices of God are a broken spirit; a broken and contrite heart, O God you will not despise'.

Psalm 51 : 17

THE PRAYER BOOK OF THE BIBLE

In Dietrich Bonhoeffer's excellent book "Psalms. The Prayer Book of the Bible" he says: "There is in the Psalms no quick and easy resignation to suffering. There is always struggle, anxiety, doubt … But even in the deepest hopelessness God alone remains the one addressed." We should realise by now that there are no shortcuts to be taken on this road marked Grief. We are like a river that will burst its banks if you try and steer it through a shorter route. It is harder than ever to grasp this in these days of instant gratification.

As we pour out our souls to God, our relationship with Him will be deepened.

"God is not a surface phenomenon, slight and changeable like moods or weather. He comes to us in the depths, sharing what is most eternal in Himself with what is most needful in us".

(Praying with the Psalms by Eugene Peterson.)

Peterson also writes: "Language is not speech, it is a full circle from word to sound to perception to understanding to feeling … and before the listener can become a listener, something has to happen to him: **he must expect.**" Note again the importance of our attitude of mind.

I personally feel that our unpredictable climate makes us in northern Europe very resilient. This may be good in some ways because we don't cave in easily. But God can speak to us much more easily when we are weak. As we pour out our souls to God, our relationship with Him will be deepened. It is so hard for us with our stiff upper lips to take in this truth, but we have much to unlearn.

O Lord, support us all the day long of this troublous life, until the shades lengthen, and the evening comes, and the busy world is hushed, the fever of life is over, and our work is done. Then, Lord, in thy mercy, grant us safe lodging, a holy rest, and peace at last; through Jesus Christ our Lord.

CHOICE - THE OFFER OF
LIFE AND DEATH

'Now what I am commanding you today is not too difficult for you or beyond your reach. It is not up in heaven, so that you have to ask, 'Who will ascend into heaven to get it and proclaim it to us so we may obey it?' Nor is it beyond the sea … no, the word is very near to you; it is in your mouth and in your heart so you may obey it.

See, I have set before you today life and prosperity, death and destruction. For I command you today to love the Lord your God, to walk in His ways, and to keep His commands, decrees and laws; then you will live and increase, and the Lord your God will bless you.

Now, choose life, so that you and your children may live and that you may love the Lord your God, listen to His voice, and hold fast to Him. For the Lord is your life.'

Deuteronomy 30 : 11

A simple choice. A serious challenge.

Death is not extinguishing a light:
It is putting out the lamp because dawn has come.

PRAISE

The most important lesson to learn is to praise God in the furnace and to look for Him in everything. It is hard enough to do this when things are going well, but well nigh impossible when you are struggling at the bottom of the pit. But it is an attitude of mind. Try going for a walk in a beautiful place and look at God's creation; lean on your friends and thank Him for them. If you have a family thank Him for them too. Or a dog; a cat; a cheery passer by who smiles at you. Praise Him for any blessing, however small. Praise Him for a nice day, praise Him for the rain, praise Him for all the years you had with your loved one. The list is endless once you start to think positively. Psalms are especially good for praise. Read them whenever you find it hard to praise the Lord.

> Give rest O Christ to thy servant with thy saints;
> Where sorrow and pain are no more;
> Neither sighing but life everlasting
> Dust thou art and unto dust shalt thou return
> And weeping o'er the grave we make our song.
> Alleluia, alleluia, alleluia.

'I will exalt you, my God and King; I will praise your name for ever and ever….. Great is the Lord and most worthy of praise; His greatness no-one can fathom.'

LOVE

No book like this is complete without a piece about love. There is such a wealth of material on hand so I am not going into it in any depth, but following on from praise (also a huge subject and one that is too much ignored) I have chosen this bitter-sweet poem because sometimes it is very hard to love when one is in the depths of despair:

Ah my angry Lord, since thou dost love, yet strike;
Cast down, yet help afford; sure I will do the like.

I will complain, yet praise;
I will bewail, approve;
And all my sour-sweet days
I will lament, and love.

George Herbert

And I pray that you, being rooted and established in love, may have power ... to grasp how wide and long and deep is the love of Christ, and to know this love surpasses knowledge.

Ephesians 3 : 18-19.

In times of darkness, love sees…
In times of silence, love hears….
In times of doubt, love hopes….
In times of sorrow, love heals….
And in all times, love remembers.
So let there be love.

JESUS

I have just found this lovely hymn which I hope will bring comfort to the broken-hearted:

I sometimes think about the cross,
And shut my eyes and try to see
The cruel nails and crown of thorns,
And Jesus crucified for me.

But even could I see Him die,
I could but see a little part,
Of that great love, which, like a fire,
Is always burning in His heart.

It is most wonderful to know
His love for me so free and sure;
But 'tis more wonderful to see
My love for Him so faint and poor.

And yet I want to love Thee, Lord,
O light the flame within my heart,
And I will love Thee more and more
Until I see Thee as thou art.

William Walsham How

I expect you have your favourite pieces and poems on love, but read St. John's Gospel for the greatest words on love from Jesus' own mouth.

> 'For God so loved the world that he gave His one and only Son, that whoever believes in Him shall not perish but have eternal life'.

John 3 : 16

DOUBT

It is perfectly normal to have a crisis of faith when someone close to us dies: we will feel very vulnerable... Why should it happen to us? we keep wondering. Are we being punished? Could we have done something to prevent it happening? We might even turn our back on God because He was not there to stop the suffering.

Turn to Psalm 73 which is masterly on faith and doubt. It tells us how easy it is to envy the lifestyle of the wicked who seem to be 'free from the burdens common to man'. We must not covet their state: it only makes us bitter.

We may well even question the value of being holy: what is the point? we ask. The only way forward is to take the problem to God. We are told that it is the wicked who are the ones on the slippery slope. I stress again the importance of realising that as Christians we are not exempt from suffering. To pretend that we do not feel the pain of misfortune or loss is not evidence of maturity, but of immaturity. We will have as much as everyone else, but God will be there with us. He never gives us more than we can bear. God is real to us in the worst of times. It is vital to understand that He is willing to let things happen to us which may be painful but which will make us more holy as a result. Our character tends to make more progress in the tough times than the good.

'But as for me, my feet had almost slipped; I had nearly lost my foothold…. When my heart was grieved and my spirit embittered, I was senseless and ignorant… yet I am always with you; you hold me by my right hand…. It is good to be near God. I have made you my refuge; I will tell of all your deeds.'

Taken from Psalm 73 : 1,23 and 28

ST. DAVID'S

BLESSED ASSURANCE

My sister-in-law sent me this after Mervyn had died, and it spoke straight into my heart:

Lord, my loved ones are near me.
My eyes can't see them because they
have left for the moment their bodies
as one leaves behind outmoded clothing....

Before, our bodies touched, but not our souls.
Now I meet them when I meet you.
I receive them when I meet you.
I love them when I love you.

Lord I love you,
and I want to love you more.
It's you who make love eternal,
and I want to love eternally.

Michael Quoist

He whom we love is no longer where he
was before; he is now wherever we are.

St. John Chrysostom

I have left some of the lines out because I felt they were verging on spiritualism which we are told in no uncertain fashion never to embrace. It is terribly tempting in times of deep depression after the death of one's loved one to try to communicate with them. Do **not** is the only advice I can give you.

THE GIFT OF TEARS

'My tears have been my food day and night'

Psalm 42 : 3

Dry not, dry not
Your tears of love eternal!
Only to eyes that fail to weep
Does this world seem dull and dead
Dread not, dry not
Those long sad tears of love.

Never be afraid to cry: tears are a gift. Every source of water is from the Lord: the efficacy of wells; of springs from below and rain from above. Also there is living water: a spring of water welling up to eternal life. So be thankful for the gift of tears.

I was given an insignificant but useful piece of practical advice to drink plenty of water, as one may be losing a lot through tears.

Give rest O Christ to thy servant with thy saints;
Where sorrow and pain are no more;
Neither sighing but life everlasting
Dust thou art and unto dust shalt thou return
And weeping o'er the grave we make our song.
Alleluia.

WEAKNESS

Give your weakness to the one who helps.
Cry out!
Don't be stolid and silent with your pain.
Lament!
And let the milk of loving flow through
into you.
The hard rain and wind are ways the cloud
has to take care of us.

STRENGTH

When I must leave you for a little while,
Please do not grieve and shed wild tears,
And hug your sorrows to you through the years,
But start out bravely with a gallant smile;
And for my sake and in my name;
Live on and do all things the same,
Feed not your loneliness on empty days,
But fill each waking hour in useful ways,
Reach out your hand in comfort and in cheer
And I in turn will comfort you and hold you near;
And never, never be afraid to die,
For I am waiting for you in the sky!

Helen Steiner Rice

PART 4 - HOPE AND ASSURANCE

I pray also that the eyes of your heart
may be enlightened in order that
you may know the
hope
to which He has called you,
the riches of His glorious
inheritance in the saints,
and His incomparably
great power for us
who believe.

Ephesians 1:18,19

THE FINAL VICTORY

However deeply we are grieving, it is important to remember that death is the gateway to the final victory. *See 1 Corinthians 15 : 26.* Of course the shock varies enormously according to how the death has occurred: if it has been sudden or traumatic; or someone before their allotted life span, especially a child. Perhaps even worse still a victim of murder, a suicide or any other misadventure or accident. I am perfectly certain that this can be compounded by bitterness, resentment, guilt or regrets. It is so important to give any of these unresolved feelings to the Lord because healing can never take place if you are harbouring unforgiveness. Remember that Christ has paid for our healing through the Cross: all we have to do is to believe that deep down in our hearts.

Christ of wounds, Christ of tears,
Christ of the wounds of the piercing,
Hold us in your hands, scarred with love,
Through all our trials and sufferings,
And by your wounds, we may find healing.

A Gethsemane Prayer

Just think of what He suffered for us, but also look at the glorious truth in *1 Corinthians 15 : 55*: 'Death has been swallowed up in victory. Where, O death, is your victory? O death, where is your sting'?
But thanks be to God who gives us the victory through our Lord Jesus Christ.

And death shall have no dominion
Dylan Thomas

44

GOD'S LENT CHILD

The closest experience of an untimely death that I have had to endure was that of Mervyn's much-loved niece who was killed in a car crash aged 32. It is hard to give comforting words at such a time, but I think this poem is wonderful for anyone who has the misfortune to lose someone close before their allotted time.

"I'll lend you for a little while
a child of mine" God said
"for you to love while he lives
and mourn for when he's dead.

He'll bring his charms to gladden you,
and, should his stay be brief,
you'll have his lovely memories
as a solace for your grief....

It may be six or seven years
or forty two or three;
but will you, till I call him back
take care of him for me"?

But should thy angels call for him
much sooner than we planned,
we'll brave the bitter grief that comes,
and try to understand.

HOPE

Sometimes Hope gets lost between the enormity of Faith and Love. It is such a very important component of the grief journey that you are on....

Take time to think of this amazing truth: At the Crucifixion, Jesus said to the penitent thief:

'This day thou shalt be with me in Paradise.'

At noon they were in this world. At 3 p.m. they were in Paradise, where they were able to recognise each other as Jesus promised.

This is the most reassuring thing that we are told in the Bible about life after death - movement from this world to Paradise, where we shall recognise and be known to each other as we are in this life.

**The life of Jesus Christ
is a message of HOPE
a message of MERCY,
a message of LIFE in a dark world.**

'A faith and knowledge resting on the hope of eternal life, which God, who does not lie, promised before the beginning of time'.

Titus 1: 2

'Therefore my heart is glad and my tongue rejoices; my body will also live in hope because you will not abandon me to the grave…'

Hope keeps us going through our faith in Jesus. Hope for being re-united with your loved one for eternity is what enables you to live life to the full until you are called to glory. Praise the Lord!

Hope of the world, thou Christ of great compassion Speak to our fearful hearts by conflict rent.
Save us, thy people, from consuming passion, Who by our own false hopes and aims are spent.

Georgina Harkness

'We have this hope as an anchor for the soul, firm and secure. It enters the inner sanctuary behind the curtain.'

Hebrews 6 : 19

GRACE

Never underestimate God's grace, which is often
overlooked in our times of strife. He is a God of grace,
hope, mercy and above all, everlasting life.
What a friend to have!

Surely these lines from John Newton's epic hymn will
make your heart soar:

"Twas GRACE that taught my heart to fear,
and grace my fears relieved;
How precious did that grace appear
the hour I first believed...

Through many dangers, toils and snares,
I have already come;
'tis grace hath brought me safe thus far,
and grace will lead me home."

God's
Riches
At
Christ's
Expense

'My grace is sufficient for you'.

2 Corinthians 12 : 9

FAITH

Faith is not faith until it is all you are holding on to.

I found huge comfort in these words of Mrs. Ewing:

"Can the last parting do much to hurt such friendship between good souls, who have so long learned to say farewell, to love in absence, to trust through silence, and to have faith in reunion?"

Help me to hold those, whom I love and have lost, in my memory with all the sadness and joy that brings.

"Give us O God something of the spirit of your servant John the Baptist: his moral courage; his contentment with simplicity; his refusal to be fettered by this world; his faithfulness in witness to the end".

From A Pilgrim's Manual by Brendan O'Malley

'Now faith is being sure of what we hope
for and certain of what we cannot see'.

Hebrews 11 : 1

Focus on your faith rather than your doubts.

'He redeemed us in order that the blessing given to Abraham might come to the Gentiles through Christ Jesus, so that by faith we might receive the promise of the Spirit.'

Galatians 3 : 14

COURAGE

I don't know where I first found this poem for the Four Graces, but it seemed to capture people's imagination.

The Queen then chose it for her Mother's Thanksgiving Service. At the time no-one knew of its provenance, but months later - through the press - it was a delight to discover that it had been written by one David Harkin:

You can shed tears that she is gone
or you can smile because she has lived.

You can close your eyes and pray that she'll come back
or you can open your eyes and see all she's left.

Your heart can be empty because you can't see her
or you can be full of the love you shared.

You can turn your back on tomorrow and live yesterday
or you can be happy for tomorrow
because of yesterday.

You can remember her and only that she's gone
or you can cherish her memory and let it live on.

You can cry and close your mind, be
empty and turn your back
or you can do what she'd want:
smile, open your eyes, love and go on.

David Harkin

This struck such a chord with me, as I think it does with most people. I felt that I was duty bound to carry on as Mervyn would have liked; I am sure that it is very important to try to be brave for the sake of our lost ones. For this reason I include the following poem, but although I have often seen it, I cannot find who wrote it:

If I should die and leave you here awhile
be not like others, sore undone, who keep
Long vigils by the silent dust and weep.
For my sake, turn again to life and smile,
Nerving the heart and trembling hands to do
Something to comfort weaker hearts than thine.
Complete those dear unfinished tasks of mine
And I perchance may therein comfort you.

Joyce Grenfell

AN EPITAPH

Even such is Time, which takes in trust
Our youth, our joys, and all we have,
And pays us but with age and dust,
Who in the dark and silent grave,
When we have wandered all our ways,
Shuts up the story of our days;
And from which earth, and grave, and dust,
The Lord shall raise me up, I trust.

Sir Walter Raleigh

LAUGHTER

Another warning of something that may catch you unawares: you may find it hard to laugh out loud on your own. You can think something is outrageously funny, but rather like talking to yourself, it is a bit strange to laugh out aloud. My goodness it helps having a dog though. I cannot recommend animals highly enough, but I am sure that everyone knows how wonderful they are when one is on one's own.

"Laugh and the world laughs with you; cry, and you cry alone" may be a rather cruel maxim to live by, but it is better as time goes on to try and keep smiling. Of course people will understand one's grief but however much one is breaking inside, it is incredibly important not to wallow in self pity. Again I stress that it is an attitude of mind.

> Special people and happy thoughts
> just seem to go together.

That man is a success who lives well, laughs often, and loves much; who gained the respect of intelligent men and the love of children; who fills his niche and accomplishes his tasks; who will leave this world better than he found it... and who looks for the best in others and gives the best he has . . .

Look at Philippians 4 : ⁴'Rejoice in the Lord always. I will say it again: rejoice' and do read on - the following five verses are gloriously poetic.

BLESSINGS

'The Lord bless you and keep you;
The Lord make his face to shine upon you
and be gracious to you.
The Lord turn his face towards you
And give you peace.'

Numbers 6 : 24-26

———·———

May the peace of the Lord Christ go with you,
wherever He may send you,
May He guide you through the wilderness,
Protect you through the storm.
May He bring you home rejoicing
At the wonders He has shown you,
May He bring you home rejoicing
Once again into our doors.

———·———

The sun will no more be your light by day,
Nor will the brightness of the moon shine on you,
For the Lord will be your everlasting light,
And your God will be your glory.
Your sun will never set again,
And your moon will wane no more;
The Lord will be your everlasting light
And your days of sorrow will end.

DEATH

Death can take away from us what we have,
But cannot rob us of who we are:
We are children of the Heavenly Father
And co-heirs with Christ to the Kingdom of Heaven.

HEAVEN

Bring us, O Lord God at our last awakening into
the house and gate of Heaven, to enter into that
gate and dwell in that house where there shall be
no darkness nor dazzling, but one equal light;
no noise nor silence, but one equal music;
no fears nor hopes but one equal possession;
no ends nor beginnings but one equal eternity,
in the habitations of Thy glory and dominion;
world without end.
Amen

John Donne, Dean of St. Paul's.

'And I heard a loud voice from the throne saying '. and
God Himself will be with them and be their God.... He will
wipe every tear from their eyes. There will be no more
death or mourning or crying or pain, for the old order of
things has passed away.'

Revelation 21 : 3-4

I hope that this sonnet by Elizabeth Barrett Browning will speak into your heart as it does into mine. Why not dedicate it to the one whom you have loved and lost:

> How do I love thee? Let me count the ways.
> I love thee to the depth and breadth and height
> My soul can reach, when feeling out of sight
> For the ends of Being and ideal Grace.
> I love thee to the level of every day's
> Most quiet need, by sun and candlelight.
> I love thee freely, as men strive for Right;
> I love thee purely, as they turn from Praise.
> I love thee with the passion put to use
> In my old griefs, and with my childhood's faith.
> I love thee with a love I seemed to lose
> With my lost saints - I love thee with the breath,
> Smiles, tears, of all my life! And, if God choose,
> I shall but love thee better after death.

Pray for me, and I shall for you,
and for all your friends,
that we may merrily meet in heaven.

Sir Thomas More

O call it not death; it is life just begun

PART 1 - THE PARTING

PART 2 - THE GRIEVING PROCESS

PART 3 - TRUST IN GOD

PART 4 - HOPE AND ASSURANCE

Cancer is so limited.
It cannot cripple love.
It cannot shatter hope.
It cannot corrode faith.
It cannot eat away peace.
It cannot kill friendship.
It cannot cut out memories.
It cannot silence courage.
It cannot invade the soul.
It cannot reduce eternal life.
It cannot quench the spirit.
It cannot lessen the power of the Resurrection.

Death is the last and greatest gift that God has
for the living.

Ingram Content Group UK Ltd.
Milton Keynes UK
UKHW041320080623
423108UK00001B/10